History and Folklore of the Cowichan Indians

by Martha Douglas Harris

with an introduction by Roger Chambers

This work contains material that was originally published in 1901.

*This publication was created and published for the public benefit,
utilizing public funding and is within the Public Domain.*

*This edition is reprinted for educational purposes
and in accordance with all applicable Federal Laws.*

Introduction Copyright 2018 by Roger Chambers

IMPORTANT NOTE & DISCLAIMER

IMPORTANT NOTE :

As with all reprinted books of this age that are intended to perfectly reproduce the original edition, considerable pains and effort had to be undertaken to correct fading and sometimes outright damage to existing proofs of this title.

At times, this task can be quite monumental, requiring an almost total rebuilding of some pages from digital proofs of multiple copies. Despite this, imperfections still sometimes exist in the final proof and may detract slightly from the visual appearance of the text.

Some images may suffer from reduced quality due to anomalies in the original scan.

DISCLAIMER :

Due to the age of this book, some methods or practices may have been deemed unsafe or unacceptable in the interim years. In utilizing the information herein, you do so at your own risk.

We republish antiquarian books with no judgment or revisionism, solely for their historical and cultural importance, and for educational purposes.

Self Reliance Books

Get more historic titles on animal and stock breeding, gardening and old fashioned skills by visiting us at:

http://selfreliancebooks.blogspot.com/

introduction

I am very pleased to present to you another wonderful old book on North American Natives – ***History and Folklore of the Cowichan Indians***. It was written by Martha Douglas Harris, and first published in 1901, making it well over a century old.

This old gem is filled with short, quick-read stories from the folklore of the Cowichan Indian people of Vancouver, British Columbia, Canada.

The book has stories including the enigmatically-titled *The Story of the First Man on Earth, Sowittan, or the Grumbler, The War Song, Stetalht, or Spirit People, Children of the Moon, Folk Lore of the Cree Indians, Chis-tapistaquhn, or the Rolling Head,* and more.

A wonderful old book on some fascinating Canadian-Indian folklore, and a must-read for all those interested in the histories of North American native tribes.

~ *Roger Chambers*

State of Jefferson, February 2018

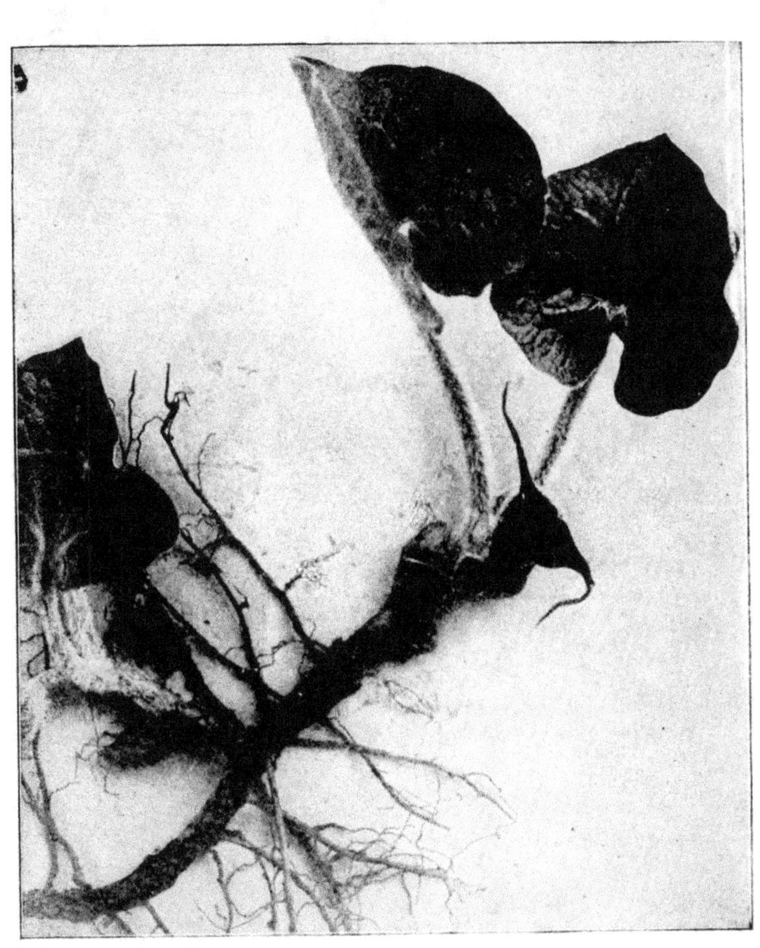

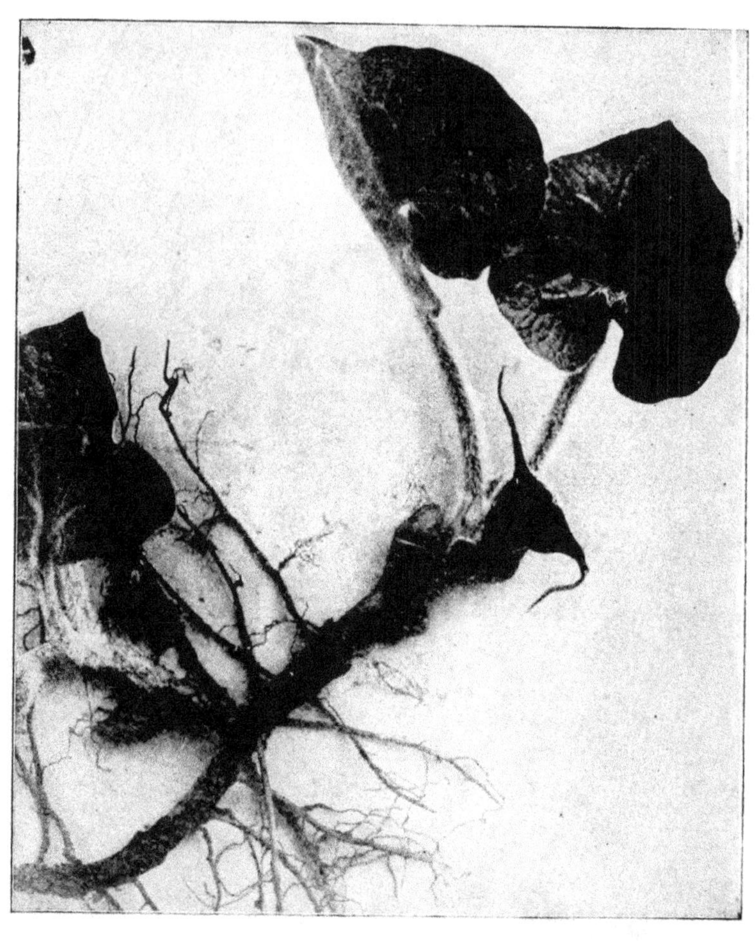

THE history and legends of the Indians of the Pacific Northwest is especially interesting from the fact that they have not been so long or so closely in touch with the white races as the other aboriginal inhabitants of North America. This little volume deals with the Cowichan tribe of Vancouver Island, who, from being a numerous and powerful people, are now reduced to a mere handful. Civilization is destroying their native dignity and wholesome life, substituting much evil for the real good found in their former customs and character. Their legends are fast being forgotton, and as a contribution towards their preservation, I have translated them as a memento of British Columbia.

M. D. H.

THE STORY OF THE FIRST MAN ON EARTH

The first man on earth was named Quiltumtun. How very happy he was; everything was so beautiful. At last he began to feel a want in his happy life; there was something wanting; there was no one to cook for him and no one to take an interest in him. So he resolved to make a companion—one like himself, only not as strong, but one who would wait for him and cook for him. He set to work to carry out his ideas. He chose a fine piece of wood; it was a yew, and after a great deal of trouble made him an image of a woman. He covered the skin with herbs and made flesh. He could scarcely keep from shouting for joy. Here at last was a friend who should help him. This wooden friend could now only nod its head and roll its eyes; there was no life in it, though the skin felt warm. How could he make it perfect?

Whilst he was so busy, he forgot to eat; and at last, being hungry, he went to his larder and found it empty, thus was compelled to go out hunting, so before leaving he made fire, and, placing the image before it, told the wooden friend that she must not let the fire go out; and, placing the materials for a basket before her, told her to finish it before he came home, so that she might keep busy till he returned

At evening, weary and worn, he returned home, to find the fire had gone out, and the basket was still unmade. The friend nodded her head and smiled, but he got angry and slapped her face. The next day he went out again, and left the same things for her to do.

The birds had carried the news of Quiltumtun's wooden wife as far as Sooke, where lived two women also alone; and when they heard of Quiltumtun they hurried to Cowichan and there found the lodge and the wooden woman sitting calmly before the remains of the fire, and also the materials for a basket before her. They set to work then and finished the basket, and set it before her, and made the fire and cooked the meat, and then hid, so as to see what Quiltumtun would do. Soon he came home, bringing a large elk with him, and what joy was his to find that his wife had been able to do so much. Oh, he was so pleased. The next day he went off again, and left another basket to be made. Then the women came in and made the basket, and put the woman on the top of the lodge. When Quiltumtun came home he looked everywhere for his wife, and at last found her. How angry he was, and asked her how she had got up there. There was no answer, and the poor fellow did not know what to make of it.

Well, the fourth time he went off hunting, the two friends came in and took the image outside, where they had made a large fire, and, throwing it in, let it burn, when it exploded with a loud noise.

That was the end of the wooden friend. They then finished the task of basket-making, and when it was near the time that Quiltumtun was in the habit of returning, they made a fire and cooked meat for him, and then hid themselves, to see what would happen. When he came home he found a bright fire burning and his supper cooking, but no wife anywhere to be seen. So he began to hunt about the lodge, inside and out, and at last found the two women, who confessed what they had done.

He liked them so well that he asked them to marry him. They lived very happily, and from them the Cowichans are descended.

SOWITTAN, OR THE GRUMBLER.

In olden times people had no canoes, as they have now-a-days, but used big logs for going about with. They had to trust to the tides and currents to take them to the islands they wished to visit. Now, there lived a man whose name was Sowittan, who lived at Chemainus. Word had come to him that at Stitless, or New Westminster, there dwelt a fair maiden, and he became so eager to see her that he determined to cross the Gulf, which was almost impassable on account of the huge and terrible serpents and fish that lived there. However, nothing daunted, Sowittan started off on his big log; but when he got to the Gulf he had to turn back, as he could not cross; so home again he came, and hunted for all the poisonous herbs he could gather, and tied them into bundles and put them on his log, and started again. This time he was successful, as he kept the monsters busy with the bundles of herbs that he threw them, and so crossed the Gulf in safety.

On the North Arm there lived a man called Hanaymult, the first man who was made there. He had a large family now, and when Sowittan came he was glad to see him. After many days' feasting and dancing, Sowittan claimed the maiden, who was glad to have such a brave husband. Sowittan now made ready for the voyage home. He collected fresh poisonous herbs and tied them on; then he and his bride sat on the log, and so off for home. The monsters tried to devour them, but the herbs had the power to quiet them, and so Sowittan crossed the Gulf safely. The currents took them into all the little bays and harbors. After this long voyage they reached home and were warmly welcomed by their friends.

One day when Sowittan was busy trying to dry fish, two men appeared coming down from the clouds. How frightened he was, but they made signs to him not to be alarmed. Then they asked him what his name was.

"Oh, it is Sowittan, or the man who grumbles."

"Why, what have you to grumble about?" said they.

"Oh, everything."

"Well, tell us them, and perhaps we can help you. Our name is Haalees, or spirit men. Now, you have a wife; you must be enjoying yourself."

"No, indeed, I have much to trouble about. You see me now trying to dry this fish; well, it is far too big, and before I have finished, it begins to decay. The herrings are all too big; everything is too large. The deer are so big that we cannot eat them, and they have to rot. Everything was made wrongly; I could do better myself. The mountains are so big I can't see over the tops, and so high that I cannot get a breath of wind from the big sea. Everything is so dry, no rain; and yet the land is so swampy that every time I take a step I almost fall in. Then I am too big too."

After Sowittan had finished his long string of troubles, the Haalees said :

"Now, Sowittan, let us go over and consult your father-in-law; perhaps he will not think as you do."

So they all went off on Sowittan's log, and went to visit Hanaymult and get his opinion. At first Hanaymult thought that everything was just right, but maybe the sturgeon were too large; in fact it was impossible to use them, so fishing was bad.

So the Haalees promised that they would make the world over again so as to suit them. They gave Sowittan a slingshot and hard black stone. "Now," said Haalees, "shoot at the mountains till you are satisfied with them."

Then he took the sling and stone and peppered away at the mountains. The tops flew off and fell into the sea with a tremendous noise; the waters boiled furiously, and up came islands; that is how there are so many islands along the coast. The fish died in the sea, and the plains were burnt up.

"Now, Sowittan, how does this please you?"

"Well, I don't know yet. I will go to the top of the hills and look if I can see the big water."

By and by he came back, quite joyfully. He was almost satisfied.

"Now for the swampy places. Take these slates and stick them in the ground, and then walk on them and see if you sink."

So Sowittan did as he was told, and to his joy the

plain was made hard so that he could walk without sinking in the earth. When he returned he said: "Haalees, this is just what I want. Make me small too, and I shall be happy."

So Haalees granted him his wish, and in an instant he grew shorter, but shouted: "Stop! Stop! I don't want to be too small."

So they made him the height that men now grow. After this the Haalees or spirits went up to Heaven. Sowittan became happy and the father of many people.

THE STORY OF THE FLOOD BY THE COWICHAN INDIANS.

In the days after "Sowittan, or the Grumbler," the people were so numerous that they spread all over the land, till the hunting became scarce. The Cowichan, Saanich, Kuper Island and Nanaimo people increased so rapidly that they began to quarrel over their boundaries. They had also increased their store of knowledge, and were becoming skilled in the art of shaping paddles, weaving baskets, dressing skins, and making dresses from cedar bark, which they wove into stout material for the purpose. The canoes were still logs, but they began to use clam-shells to shape them with. They were blunt at both ends, just like scows.

They also had wise men, who had power to foretell the future, and these men were greatly troubled on account of certain dreams, which foretold destruction of the people, if they were true. One man said, "I have dreamed a strange thing," and the others were eager to hear what he had to say. "I dreamed that such rain fell that we all were drowned."

"I," said another, "dreamed that the river rose and flooded the place, and we were all destroyed."

"So did I," chimed in another. "And I too."

They could not understand what these dreams could mean; so they called a council to decide what they had better do. At last they decided to build a huge raft of many canoes tied together, the like of which was never seen before. So they set to work, amidst the jeering of the people who would not believe in these dreams. After many months they finished the raft and tied it with long cedar-bark ropes and made a huge rope of cedar bark that could reach the top of Cowichan Mountain, where they passed it through the middle of a huge stone, to serve as the anchor. The stone is still there, as a witness of the truth. They were a long time at work. At length all was ready. The raft floated in Cowichan Bay, a wonderment to all about. Not long afterwards the rain commenced. The drops were as large as hailstones, and so heavy that they killed the little babies. The river rose and all the valleys were covered. People took refuge in the mountain, but that was soon under water. When the rain began, the wise people, and the friends who believed, took their families and placed them on the raft and took food and waited. By and by the raft rose with the water, and was the only thing seen for many days. How terrified they all were, and could not divine why this terrible calamity had been sent for.

They prayed to the Great Spirit for help, but none came.   As the rain fell, they were kept busy bailing out the rain with their cedar-bark bailers.   At length the rain stopped, and they felt the waters going down, and their raft rested on the top of Cowichan Mountain, being held by the anchor and cedar rope.   Then they saw land, but what desolation met their eyes ! How their hearts were wrung with anguish !   It was indescribable, but they took courage and landed, and went to where their old homes had been.   They began to rebuild the village and take up their old life again. After this they increased rapidly, and soon filled their lands with people.   Then they quarrelled among themselves so bitterly that they agreed to separate, and in this way was the world peopled.

HISTORY OF THE COWICHANS.

This war that I am about to relate took place about 300 years ago.   The Cowichans had grown a great and powerful people, numbering many thousands. They had been insulted, or some of their friends had been killed by the people of Snohomish, now in American territory.   Now, they were burning to avenge this deed, and mustered their fighting men and manned their war canoes, and off they started. They got safely across the Sound and attacked the people of Snohomish, conquered them and burnt their villages.   From there they went on to Port Manson, and then to Colthic, a village near Port

Townsend, and on to Los Angeles, conquering wherever they went.   After an absence of a month they turned homewards, laden with the spoils of war; but what was their horror on reaching home, where they expected a warm welcome, to find their villages all in ruins and their wives and children gone.   An old man hobbled down to the beach and told them of what had taken place.   The Fort Rupert and one hundred and twenty Northern tribes had come down on a war expedition, and had fallen on the defenceless villages of Cowichan, Kuper Island and Saanich, and had killed the men left in charge and carried off the women and slaves, to be " elitans," or slaves.   The Cowichans did not wait long, but hurried to the New Westminster people and asked their help.   They are related to the Cowichans.   The Songhees, who lived at Metchosin, sent word to say that the Northern tribes were going to make a second foray, and try to carry off the men this time.   The Songhees bid their friends wait till the Northern people came down.

One day a small canoe came flying with the news that the invaders were coming.   About 300 canoes had passed Nanaimo.   So the Cowichans and New Westminsters went to meet them.

At Maple Bay the invaders had landed to rest. The Cowichans crept up and waited outside of the bay.   In order to draw the enemy out to sea, they sent a canoe, with a man disguised as a woman, and twenty men lying at the bottom of the canoe, fully armed and covered with mats, across the entrance of the harbor.   When the Northern people saw this, they pushed off and went in chase of the canoe.   The canoe turned out to sea and drew the people after it; and, when well out, the Cowichan, Saanich and New

Westminster contingents gave chase, and then the battle commenced. The Northern people were surrounded and kept in for two days and three nights. The water was red with blood. The Cowichans sang their war song, given by Stimqua, the great snake, which fell from Heaven into the bay. At last a few canoes escaped and were chased as far as Comox. They were upset and the people killed. Not one of the North people escaped.

After resting, the Cowichan, Kuper Island and Saanich people went to look for their wives and children. They were successful, and brought them home safely. Then they made a second expedition for revenge, burning the villages and taking the women and children captive. This broke the power of the North people, and the Cowichans lived in peace for many years.

THE WAR SONG.

This great snake, Stimqua, fell into the harbour, and the people were so alarmed that they did not know what to do.

" Come, let us kill this monster, and he will be in our power."

So the brave men of the tribe got into their canoes and surrounded the snake and killed it, and dragged the huge monster to the foot of the Cowichan Mountain. The rope was made of cedar bark. This

is the song that was made to commemorate the event:
The spear that killed Stimqua was poisoned with his
blood, and his spirit came on the people.

    Song—Only sung when going to battle:
        If we only shake our spear at you
        And shout "Whow!" you die.
      We are the Cowichans,
        Stimqua is our power.

THE STORY OF QUAMICHAN.

A wild woman named Quamichan, who made a
basket out of a snake, was a giantess, and her whole
appearance was disgusting. She lived on human
flesh, and sneaked about villages, stealing the children, which she put into her snake basket. She lived
on Salt Spring Island, near Kuper. She had wings
and used to fly about Saanich and elsewhere, stealing
young people. Her sister was a very small woman,
and hated Quamichan bitterly. Quamichan decided
to have a big feast and invite her friends; so for a
few days she was kept busy stealing children, whom
she hid in a cave. When she had enough, she dug a
huge pit, about 100 feet square and very deep. She
put big sticks across the top, and between she placed
small dry wood as kindlings, and then big stones on
the top of all. Then she set fire to the wood. She
called the children out, and made them sit down and
watch the fire. There were hundreds of poor children, crying and begging to be let go home. She made

fire by rubbing two sticks together in this fashion: A flat stick with a small hole in the middle, and a small round stick with a sharp point to fit in the flat piece of wood; then the round stick was rubbed violently between the two palms, and as soon as smoke and sparks were seen coming out, fine dry cedar bark was held to the sparks, and as they fell on the bark it was gently blown, and the fire fanned into flame.

Now, after the fire had started, Quamichan danced round the pit, singing and shouting. "Now I am going to have a big feast with my friends, and eat these young animals," as she called the children. " I hope the stones will get red-hot quickly, so that they will be well cooked."

She told her sister to take pitch pine and make the children open their eyes, and smear their eye-balls with the pitch, so that they could not see what was going to happen.   Now, the sister's heart was tender. She took the pitch and went to each child and bid it close its eyes and put the pitch on the lids, and said to each: " When I call out ' Open your eyes!' you must get sticks and be ready, for I am going to punish Quamichan.   Now, be ready."

When she had finished, Quamichan told her to take out the sticks and throw them to one side, as the stones were red-hot.

" Yes, sister," she said; " but first dance again and sing, for you sing so well; and shut your eyes tight and look up as you dance."

Quamichan was greatly pleased with this flattery, and danced away like mad.   The little sister now got a long pole, and, when Quamichan came close by her, she thrust the pole between her legs and tripped her, and Quamichan fell into the hot pit on her back. She screamed to her sister to help her out.

"Oh, yes, I am helping you out, but you are awfully heavy; call on the boys and girls to help."

"With that the sister shouted: "Children, open your eyes," and they took sticks and threw them into the pit, where they caught fire. Quamichan was burning like oil, and the sparks from her turned into ducks, geese and all sorts of birds. This was the end of Quamichan. The little sister sent the poor children back to their homes rejoicing. The Cowichan Indians called themselves Quamichans, after this big woman, and they learnt to make fire from her.

SCALLIGHAN; OR, THE THUNDER AND LIGHTNING BIRD.

On Valdez Island there lived a large family. The eldest brother was married, but had only one child—a boy, a most strange child. As soon as he was able to walk, he went by himself into the forest, and would remain away all day and return at night. His mother would place the choicest pieces of meat before him, but in vain; a morsel of deer's fat would last him a week. His mother asked the child why it was he had no appetite for the good things she laid before him. He replied: "The lovely, sweet smell of the morning wind, full of the odor of sweet flowers and trees, is food enough for me."

Not long after this the boy failed to come home, so his father and uncles started out in search of him. They asked thousands of people if they had seen the child, but all said they had not. The poor parents grieved for five years, and one morning early, as was her custom, the mother went outside and sat down to mourn for her lost son. All at once she fancied she heard his voice calling her. How could it be? The child was dead, but the voice came nearer, and she listened to what it was saying. The song he sang was this: "My father and mother, look up now. I have come back to you. I have seen all the world. Comfort yourselves, for I still live."

The poor mother could not believe her ears. "If you are my son, show yourself to me."

"Alas! I cannot, as the day has dawned. But look up, mother, and you will see a number of little flies. I am there. If you wish to see me, mother, come out before the dawn, and I will be able to show you that I am your son." With that the voice ceased.

The mother ran in and awakened her husband "Our son has returned, and I have heard his voice."

How joyful they were, and longed for the next morning. It was the longest day they had seen.

The next day, before the dawn, both were outside waiting for the son, who came out of the forest. A shining light was about, and he looked so grand. They were afraid—surely that beautiful being was not their son. He ran up and kissed them, and after a long talk he told his father to build him a new house, made of "sliquis," or bullrushes. These rushes are made into fine mats, which are used for lining the lodges. These mats were to be perfectly new, and the house was to be immense and some dis-

     THE CHIEF'S DAUGHTER.

tance from the village; it was also to be without a roof.

Now, when the dawn broke, he disappeared, and the parents set about at once to build this large house. They called their people and all helped. At last they had ten acres enclosed in the "sliquis" mats. When all was ready they waited for the son to come and live in the new dwelling. With the dark he came, revealing himself in all his splendour. He related his adventures. He said that the last day he had wandered by himself into the forest, a monster bird, or Thunder, had carried him away, and that the bird had taken his eyes out and changed them, and had called him "Scallighan," which means "I am a great man— I have great powers and rule the spirits." Now Scallighan always kept his eyes shut, and his parents asked him the reason why.

"If I opened my eyes, the lightning would strike and kill you. I dare not show my eyes, and if I take off my hat the thunder comes." He was a terrible power.

Scallighan asked his father which was the highest mountain on the island. His father said that Salt Spring Island was the highest. "I will go there, and do you make me a large house there, as I do not like this place; it is too near the people."

So the father and five uncles went to work and pulled the mats down and carried them to Salt Spring Mountain, and there put up the house. When it was ready, Scallighan came down, and was pleased with the new house. "Now, father, I wish to marry, so go to Nanaimo and ask the Chief for his daughter. First take off my hat carefully and cover it well, so that no one sees it."

Now, the hat was very peculiar looking, and had four eagles' feathers stuck round it.

"Shew the Chief my hat if he refuses to let my daughter come with you; show only a little of it, and you will see what happens."

So the father and uncles went off in their canoes to Nanaimo, to ask the Chief there for his daughter.

When they asked for the young girl, the Chief was very angry, and demanded why the son did not come himself to ask for his daughter. They might go away again. Then Scallighan's father said :

"Here is my son's hat; if I show it to you, there will be much danger. You had better let the maid come with us."

The Chief was enraged, and scoffed at the power of the hat.

So the father uncovered a little of the hat, and then the thunder and lightning came and burnt up the Chief's house; and the old father quickly covered the hat, lest the people should be killed. How frightened were all around, and the Chief at once gave his daughter, and told them to be gone. So they went home and took the bride with them. The father restored the hat to Scallighan, who was rejoiced with his bride. He himself was invisible to her.

The neighbouring tribes, hearing of these wonderful doings, brought their daughters as peace offerings to Scallighan. There were two hundred young women in the vast lodge of Scallighan. Now, there was no roof over the lodge, so that when he opened his eyes the lightning went up and did no harm. People were terrified, and begged that Scallighan might be destroyed; but how could they kill the man who had such power, and who could become invisible.

At last two brothers who lived in Cowichan determined to rid the land of thunder and lightning, and made preparations for their warfare. They put on their war dresses, and each carried a magic sword, made out of elk horn. It had wonderful powers.

Now, the spirits told Scallighan that the two men were coming to kill him, so he waited for them. After a long climb they reached the house of sliquis, and called aloud for Scallighan to come out and show himself, so that they might fight. Scallighan replied: "I am here; come this way." So the two men went in the direction of the voice. They saw no one. Suddenly Scallighan opened his eyes and took off his hat and what a terrible storm took place ! The lightning killed the younger brother, and as he fell, the elder seized the body and held it as a shield, and went on to give battle. Scallighan became visible, and the two fought. At last the magic sword struck Scallighan and killed him, and his spirit flew off as a great bird. The young conqueror released all the wives from this huge lodge, and they all went to their old homes.

Whyuctan Swalamesett, or Tom James, and his family come from this country, and it is called "Taatka."

THE ADVENTURES OF A YOUNG MAN WITH CROOKED EYES.

A young man, who was so unfortunate as to be born with squint eyes, and who had been made the butt of the village, fell in love with the Chief's

       ZOOHALITZ.

daughter, and wished to marry her. After many weeks of torture, she refused him, as he was so ugly.

Nothing daunted, he went in search of a wise woman who lived some distance away. When he got to the place, she already knew what he had come for. "Ah, my son, so you wish something from me?"

" Yes, my mother and I am so unhappy. The maiden I wish to marry will not have me because my face is so ugly. Now, can you give me something to change my face and put my eyes straight?"

" No, my son; but do what I tell you, and you may yet be all right and get your wife. Your grandfather can help you. Well, where does he live ? "

" It is a long way, and the way is full of peril."

" Now, take with you a sack of red paint and one of deer's fat. Then go as far as the mountain you see yonder; cross that, and then be careful—you will see three mountains; keep far from them, but they are part of your way; when you have safely passed them you will come to a large plain, as big as the sea, and in the middle you will see smoke coming out. Go there and you will see your grandfather at work. He is a very wise man."

" Thank you, my mother ; I will do anything for you when I come back."

So off the youth went, got the red paint and deer's fat, and early the next day he went off to seek for his new face. After a long, toilsome journey he reached the plain, and there in the middle was a huge cloud of smoke coming. So on he hastened, till he at length stood before the smoke, and then looked down the hole and saw an old, old man at work, carving wood.

" Good day, grandfather; what are you doing ? "

" Oh, I am making wooden faces. Come in. So you are the grandson that I heard was coming to me. Well, you are not handsome; perhaps I can help you."

Then the youth produced the red paint and deer's fat.

" Just things I have been wishing for!" exclaimed the old man. " Now I can ao what you wish."

" Well, I want a new face, with straight eyes," said the youth. " Can you do that for me ? "

" Oh, yes. Now, look here," picking up a mask, " Will this do ? "

" No, indeed; it is not nice at all."

So mask after mask was shown. None would suit. At length a small cedar box was brought and opened. In it lay a very handsome wooden face.

" Now, I will have that one."

" Very well, my son; sit down and let me put it on for you."

So the youth sat down. The old man took the boy's forehead in one hand and the chin in the other, and in an instant the old face was off. After an application of deer's fat the handsome face was put on.

" Now, look at yourself in this water."

What a joyful sight met the young man's eyes ! How he shouted and danced for joy when he saw how he had been transformed ! His first thought was to go straight home; so, thanking his grandfather and wishing him good-bye, he started.

" Not so fast, my son. There are many dangers before you. Now, be careful when you reach the three mountains, for there lives a giantess, who, if she sees you, will eat you up.   Keep as far away as you can without losing your way."

So the youth went off, full of joy, and in his hurry forgetting what the old man had said.   Just as he was passing the three mountains, great was his horror on beholding an enormous woman coming to meet him.   He tried to escape, but with one stride she was by him.

"Where are you running to, my little husband?"

It was the giantess, Zoohalitz, and she snatched up the poor fellow in her arms and almost smothered him with her foul breath and kisses.   She took him to her cave, and called her slave Cheetyan.

"Here, Cheetyan, get warm water and wash your brother-in-law."

So the poor fellow had to submit.   After more torture and kissing, Zoohalitz began to yawn, and the young man jumped into her mouth and down into her stomach, where he played sad havoc with her heart; he tried to twist it and so kill his tormentor.

"How ill I am," cried Zoohalitz.   "Send for the doctor and my friends, for I feel I am going to die."

So word was sent to her friends.   They were wolves, bears, panthers, etc., and the doctor was an immense squid.   When he arrived, Zoohalitz opened her mouth.   She was in terrible agony.   For five days the young man had been her unwilling tenant. The squid thrust his long feeler down into Zoohalitz's stomach, but he could not catch the young man, who hid himself behind the heart.   So the squid had to give up trying, and the crane was sent for.   The crane pushed his long bill down her throat and tried to catch the youth, but the latter caught hold of the crane's bill and squeezed it with all his might, and

(Copyrighted.)   Some of the Ten Brothers on the Lookout for Sea Lion.

braced himself against the sides of the stomach, so that Dr. Crane could not pull his bill out. Such struggling there was. At length the youth let go of the bill, and over went the crane, rolling head over heels, and how sore was his poor bill! At last Zoohalitz was killed. But the trouble was how to get the young man out. Finally Cheetyan decided to cut Zoohalitz open, which she promptly did, and out bounded the youth. How glad he was to be free once more. He thanked his deliverer, and found out that she had been kept as a prisoner; so the young man asked her to marry him, and together they would go back to the village. So off they went, and at length reached home. How astonished the people were at seeing the young man come back looking so handsome. They could scarcely believe that it was the same ugly fellow.

Now the Chief's daughter came to see the wonder, and fell straightway in love with the young fellow. He turned from her, and would not even look at her. So she, in despair, consulted the old wise woman, who directed her to the same place as she had sent the young man, but failed to tell her to take red paint and deer's fat. So the poor maid toiled over the mountains and at length stood before the old man, who asked her what she needed, and she told him; so off came her face, and in its place did he put the young man's discarded face, squint eye and all. How miserably the poor girl felt when she saw the horrible change; but it was punishment for her treatment of her lover. She went back, but was flouted by all, and died after much misery.

THE STORY OF TEN BROTHERS AND THE SEA LION.

Once upon a time there lived near Cowichan a family of ten brothers, who were noted for deeds of daring and skill in spearing sea lions. Not far off there lived a rival family, consisting of five brothers. They were terribly jealous of the ten brothers, as they could never secure any good sea lion hunting as long as the ten brothers lived. The sea lions frequented a rocky island not far from Cowichan, and at early dawn the ten brothers were there, waiting to kill the sea lions. Now, these five brothers became greatly enraged and took counsel together as to the best means of killing these rivals. One of the brothers suggested a visit to Soo-ol-li-che, a very wise man, gifted with magic powers and ability to understand animal talk. So off they went to Soo-ol-li-che and told him their troubles and how they wished to get rid of the hateful ten brothers.

Well what would they give him as a reward ? A canoe ?

No.

Skin-blankets, etc.?

At last they said they would give him their young kinswoman, a very pretty young woman.

Yes, that would do. So he took them away to a salt lake that lies on the top of a mountain on Lopez Island, and there he made them cut down a large cedar tree; also make a passage from the lake to the sea. Soo-ol-li-che now carved the wood into a sea lion he hollowed it out, made the heart, lungs, liver, etc., of herbs, which he put into it, and then rubbed herbs over the outside. The skin grew immediately. For the whiskers he took long cedar twigs and stuck them round the mouth. The real sea lion has beautiful silver-looking whiskers, which are greatly prized, and which are used to ornament the head-dresses of the chiefs. Now the wooden animal looked just like the real thing.

When everything was ready, See-ol-liche gave the sea lion his orders. First he had to dive into the salt lake and find the passage to the sea, as the brothers had failed to find it; then it was to go to the rocky island and play about as the others did, and attract the attention of the ten brothers. They would try to spear him, and when the spears were fast in, then he was to start north and carry the young men with him. Then the sea lion plunged in the lake and came out in Cowichan harbor. Then he swam to the rocky island and there played about. The brothers were, as usual, waiting for sport, and they instantly manned their canoes to go after the lion.

"Stop! Stop!" said the elder brother, taking a good look at the animal. "That is no real sea lion; that is not real. Our enemies must have been at work, and that means mischief to us."

The other brothers, however, begged him to try to spear the animal. He was the strongest and most expert of the brothers, and to make sure of the lion, they gave him their spears. The first spear was well planted, and the cedar line given to one of the brothers; then all ten were thrust in, and the sea lion, which had been pretending to be in a dying state, now rushed off, towing the canoes and brothers with him, away out to sea and up north. They made every effort to throw the lines away. They had grown fast to their hands; they cut the lines, which grew immediately, so they gave up the struggle in despair. After many days the sea lion came to a large mountain that rose straight out of the sea, and the face of it was full of holes. Into the largest the sea lion scrambled and pulled the ten brothers after him. How terrified they were, and sore and hungry. In this huge cave there were naked men and women, and the chief of them came to the sea lion and asked him how it was he had brought these strangers in. They could not feed them, so they had better be drowned.

The people crowded around and examined the brothers' clothes, and even took them off and tried them on. These were the spirits of the sea lions.

After a year's slavery the chief allowed the brothers to go home. They were put in their canoes and told to go as far out to sea as they could before turning a certain point where lived a giant, who would eat them if he saw them. Two young sea lions were ordered to show them the way, and towed the canoes away out to sea.

Now the eldest brother was keen to see the giant, and, not regarding the advice of the sea lions or heeding his brothers' entreaties, he paddled as close as he dared to the point. "If the giant comes, I will shoot him with my arrows and kill him."

Now, this giant, Nemokis, was watching for them and when they came close enough he waded out to them and seized their canoes and dragged them in to shore. Then he ordered them into his cave. There they were kept as close prisoners. It was a gruesome place, and in the centre lay a huge flat stone, and on it the fire burned, and near it was a basket.

"Now," said Nemokis, "yonder is my wife." They looked everywhere for a woman, but he was pointing to a round basket half filled with blood.

"Take good care of that basket, or my wife will scream if you try to escape. Keep her not too warm or too cold or she will scream, and I'll beat you. Now mind, for I am going to hunt."

Such trouble they had with Nemokis' wife. The least attempt at an escape she began to scream so loudly that the giant heard her, and rushed back.

"What is it?"

"Oh, nothing," said one. "I only put her too close to the fire."

"Oh, well, be careful what you do."

One of the brothers became a great favorite with the basket wife, who allowed him to carry her about the cave. A year or more passed and they were still slaves. They were dying to escape, but how could they manage it without that wretched thing screaming? The only thing to do was to kill the horrid thing. So they collected huge flat stones and arranged how they should use them. The favourite brother was to put the basket on the flat stone and sing to it, and then the rest would dash their flat stones on it. So he carried the basket, as it had begun to whimper, and hushed it; then placed it on the flat stone, still singing; then stepped aside, when a flat stone was dropped right into the centre of the basket, and the blood splashed everywhere. So in this way was the giant's wife killed. The stones were all thrown on the first one, and such a scrambling for the opening of the cave ! There they found only two canoes, but they had to do the best they could. How swiftly they pulled away to get out of reach of the giant. They had just passed into deep water and beyond the fatal point, when they heard the giant calling to them. He was striding after them. They then redoubled their efforts. One of them, looking back, saw the giant sinking in the water up to his chin, but he turned back and got where he could throw stones at them, but they shook their paddles at him and shouted derisively at him to come and catch them. He roared so loudly that he shook the earth, and tore trees up by the roots and flung them at the canoes, so as to break them and drown the fugitives. They at last escaped, and after five years of wandering reached home, to find their village a ruin and their friends gone.

THE STORY OF SEMMELTH.

The Indian chief, Statloth, and his wife lived many years without being blessed with children, but at last the great spirit sent them a beautiful boy— the joy and pride of their lives. As he grew beyond babyhood, they found that he was only content to roam in the forest by himself. No children were ever taken as his companions. All day would the child be absent. At nightfall, however, he would return. His parents could not make out this strange silent child. At last his father followed him one day, and after a long hunt Statloth tracked his son as far as Shawnigan Lake, where, in a clear space, he saw his son playing with an immense wolf. How frightened he was ! He dared not move, for fear they would see him, and the charm would be spoilt, as the wolf was evidently a great power. So the father watched the two playing, and then crept away as silently as he could. When he got back to Saanich and his wife, he told her what a marvel he had seen. " Oh, my wife, our son is destined to become a great chief ; the Great Spirit has taken him and put his spirit in the child. Now, when our son comes back do not say anything to him, and ask him not where he has been these many days."

The evening of the next day the young son appeared and brought deer's flesh in abundance, and told his father that in future he need not go to the forest to hunt, as he was able now to keep them supplied with food.

When the lad had reached his sixteenth year, he bade his father call all his kinsmen to a big feast, so word was sent to New Westminster, Semiahmoo (or Mud Bay), Cowichan, Kuper Island, Salt Spring Island, Chemainus and Nanaimo that Chief Statloth would give a feast in honor of his son, and also that the son might receive a name. Indian children do not receive names till they reach a certain age. The lad told his father not to trouble himself about getting food, as his own friends would bring in what he wished. The day before the feast the mother was getting anxious as to where the food was to come

   CHIEF STATLOTH AT SHAWNIGAN
LAKE.

from. During the night wolves from all parts came to Saanich, each carrying a deer slung over his back. Five thousand wolves were employed in this service, and such a mountain of deer-meat was never seen before or since. Chief Statloth was so terrified at hearing the wolves that he shut the lodge door fast, and could scarcely be persuaded to come and look at the meat. At last he came out, and such a sight met his eyes ! His beloved son standing by the side of a huge wolf, who kept guard of the boy. The wolf then spoke to the father.

" Oh, chief, this, your child, has been taken by our chief to be his son, and he wishes him to be called Semmelth. He is to be a very great warrior, and our future king." With that the wolf bounded away to the forest.

During the day the visitors and guests began to arrive, and all were taken up to see this wonderful sight. Their wonder and amazement, also fear, cannot be described. When they had all come, then the cooking and feasting commenced. They ate till they nearly burst, then slept, and continued eating till the mountain of flesh had been consumed. Then the ceremony of christening the young man took place. When the people heard that he was to be called Semmelth, which was not a tribal name, they murmured and asked the reason why he should have such a name. So the young man told the reason and the story of his adoption by the wolves, and how they had given him power over all men and animals.

" Now," said Semmelth, "call upon me if you wish to go to war, and I will, by myself, conquer your enemies."

They laughed at him, but he begged them to let him show his powers. Now, they had a grudge against the Quatsino tribe, but the latter in the old days numbered thousands of people, and the Cowichans and their friends were rather afraid of attacking them ; but, inspired by the words of Semmelth, they called a war council and decided to attack the Quatsinos. They made their preparations and got their war canoes ready, and, with Semmelth as head of the expedition, started off. After eighteen days' paddling they reached Quatsino Sound.

" Now, my friends," said Semmelth, "I wish you to remain in your canoes, as I am going to kill these, our enemies, by myself. Don't follow, but wait till I call you."

So off he started, and not long after they heard such howling and baying of wolves, and then the screams of men and women. The people were being chased by wolves, pulled down and destroyed. It was a terrible scene. This carnage went on all day, and at night all was quiet. Then they took heart and crept into the village. Oh, what an awful sight met their eyes ! All the people were killed except the children. These had been spared. After burning the dead, they fed the children and left them to go back to the canoes and wait for Semmelth. He did not return, and after long waiting they went home and there found him. Semmelth had run all the way. His running was like a wolf's for swiftness, and his strength was enormous. They asked the hero how he had conquered the Quatsinos.

" Oh," said he, " my good brothers, the wolves, did the deed for me."

Then the people feared him greatly, and his fame went all over the world. The time came when he desired to marry.

"My father, I hear that Chief Heachwistan has a very fine daughter, and I would like to marry her."

So, after much talking and voyaging, the maiden was brought to Saanich and given to Semmelth as his wife. The maiden did not like her husband, and ran away from him and took a canoe and paddled back to her father. The second wife came from Salt Spring Island, and the day after the great wedding feast Semmelth did not rise, so his father went to call him, but no answer from Semmelth, and on looking at his son he found that Semmelth's throat had been cut, that the young wife had escaped, and that she had done the deed. Now, it happened that the second wife was a young man dressed as a woman and had been used by Semmelth's enemies to destroy the great wolf man.

Poor old Statloth was heart-broken—his only son to meet such a terrible death. So to the forest he went, after putting the body in a box, and that into a tree, and called for the great wolf, so that he might have revenge. On his way back the poor old man was met by a bear, and killed and eaten.

The poor mother was now by herself. One morning early she heard scratching sounds at her door, and, getting up, what should she see but a large wolf, who leaped on her, licked her face and whined, expressing as much joy as he could. Then he spoke.

"Oh, my mother, I am your son, Semmelth, and have now become a great chief over the wolves. You will never want for meat till you die, for every day

  STETALHT.

I will bring you food.   I will watch over you, so don't be afraid any more, for we are all about you." With these words he ran to the forest.

The mother never had to beg meat from any of her people, and when she died she was taken to the woods by her son and buried, wolf fashion.

Not long after this the Nootka Indians heard that Semmelth was dead, so they came to dance and burn Semmelth's village in Saanich; but the Saanich people had rushed into the woods, and the Nootkas were having a splendid dance, when down came the wolves and chased them into their canoes.   The people were so alarmed that they paddled off, and got as far as Chemainus, and there camped, when down came the wolves, killing numbers of the people.   The rest pushed off and went on to Nanaimo, where they landed, and the wolves chased them again, this time leaving only a few people alive. At last they reached home, and there the wolves came down on them and killed every one.   Thus was Semmelth revenged.

STETALHT, OR SPIRIT PEOPLE.

The Stetalht are a strange people, who can make themselves invisible.   They are almost like spirits, and only appear at night.   Their signs are scarcely known, but their whistling is heard all over the forest.   They are supposed to live in caves.   When the Indians hear these whistlings they take their guns and shoot at where the sounds come from.   One evening the chief, Stellowalth, was going down to the river by himself, and he met a strange man. On asking who he was that dared to come so near his village, the stranger answered :

"I am one who belongs to the Stetalht, and I am now come to punish you, oh, Stellowalth, for shooting at my people."

Thereupon he commanded Stellowalth to sit down. The chief had to obey. He then stripped him of his feathers and furs, and stuck the chief's body full of sharp arrows.

Two other wild people came up. "Don't kill him," said they; "you have done enough to him; let him go now."

So they ordered the chief to stand, and then to dance, and at last they let him go. Chief Stellowalth had been hypnotized by these people. Though he could hear them talk, he could not move unless they ordered him to. Then he had to promise that never again would he allow his people to shoot into the woods when they heard the whistlings.

Two Indians who had gone down to see if their salmon net was full, began to pull it into their canoe. No fish came, but at the bottom of the net lay a beautiful wild woman, dressed in fine furs, and over her face she held a large piece of white moss. They were so alarmed at seeing her that they almost dropped the net. She made signs not to be afraid. Then they took her out, and, in spite of being in the water, her clothes were not wet. Then they took her to the village. How they crowded round her and examined her. She smiled at them, and made signs that she was hungry and would like to eat. So they brought her fish and meat. When she had satisfied her hunger, she signed that she wished to remain with them. So they consented, and as long as she stayed in the village there was always plenty, for her people every night brought deer and game and placed it at her lodge door. By and by she learned to speak their language, and after a year's service said that she must leave them, and she begged them to give her a hatchet, knife and matches. She thanked them for their kindness to her, and during the night she slipped away, and they saw her no more.

In the village of Snohqualmith, after the big fishing had been done, everybody was pleased and ready to sing and dance. The chief sent word that he was going to give a big feast and dance, so the people came in numbers with their families. Such rejoicing while all this feasting and dancing was going on. A very old man—too old to enjoy such feasting, lay in his bed in his lodge. While looking up at the smoke-hole he saw a hand and arm come through and seize a dried salmon. What could it mean? Without waiting for more fish to be taken, the old man took a long fishing pole, with hook attached, and just waited for the thief. Presently the hand and arm came down again. With a dexterous handling of the fishing pole, the arm was hooked, and down fell one of the wild people. The old man tied him securely, in spite of his signs and struggles, and took him away to the lodge where they were dancing. Now the dancing had been going on for three days and nights, and the air was anything but sweet. The poor Stetalth almost died at the smell, and covered his face with moss so that he might not die.

The dance stopped and the chief came forward and was told about the capture. He asked the captive what he could do ; so the wild man raised his hand and caused the chief to stand with his mouth open and perfectly powerless, and then did the same with the people, and took what he wished and left.

These Stetalth are supposed to steal children, and the Indians are very much afraid of them.

CHEE-CHEE-KA.

Hyas ankutte, icht soyka, yaka mamook icht schilt, kopa klip chuck; pe yaka mitlite atshim, yaka nanitch okook schilt.

Tenas lele, yaka nanitch atshim, icht-ickta klatawa kopa schilt; pe yaka hyas kwutl, yaka schilt, pe yaka iskum yaka klisumtum, pe yaka nanitch icht tenas stikya.

Pe yaka wawau, "ichta mika mamook, kopa nika schilt?" Tenas stikya wawau, "Nika tikegh tlap quitsi." "Mika kopet; mika mesahchie pos kapswalla nika quitsi."

Chee-Chee-Ka mamook iskum tenas stikyas kopa yaka stehue, yaka mamook memaloost, pe qualo yaka squani, okook tenas. In-a ti, icht hyas stikya, wawau.

" Kla-how ya ! Halo mika nanitch nika tenas?" Pe-Chee-Chee-Ka, wawau. " Halo nika nanitch kah yaka. Pe okook stikya, wawau konoway yaka sikhs. Kalu, Chetwoots, mowitch, pe swaawa,

Quinass, pe klextimist konoway sikhs, pos ela han yaka—pe konoway kulakula. Halo klaska cumtux kah okook tenas mitlite.

Stikya wawau kopa, "Chea-Chea, halo mika nanitch nika tenas ?" Nika tumtum hiyu kwass kloonass yaka memaloost. "Nawitka," Chee-Chee wawau. Hyas kull pos nika nanitch, nika mamook killipi. Tenas lele okook Chea-Chea-Ka wawau. "Klonass, nika klap yaka."

Yaka hyou cumtux kah okook tenas mitlite. Pe Chee-Chee-Ka, hyou mamook temanous, konamoxt yaka olukats, pe quietan ats. "Coolie konaway Kah Tipsoo pos nanitch tenas stikya." Pe yaka coolie konaway illi-hi, pe halo. Alta Chee-Chee-Ka cultus wawau, yaka mamook squalish, copa yaka ats. Pe yaka iskum okook tenas stikya. Yaka memaloost, yaka mash yaka qualo, konamoxt yaka schyus. "Nah, nanitch mika tenas!" Alta konaway stikya tillicum hyu haam.

Pos-kahta mika mamook mamcloos niska tenas? Alta konaway tillicum coolee pos iskum Chee-Chee-Ka pe wake kahta pos iskum. Chee-Chee-Ka klatawa killipi, copa quietan illi-hi, yaka ipsoot copa scholtz pe winapie yaka chachow copa klahanie, pe hyou enyalish.

Tenas lele, Scattle, mamook iskum Chee-Chee-Ka pe tillicum hyou melalum. Pe sciekikwas wawau, "Chee-Chee-Ka, nika sikhs, halo memaloost okook soyka, yaka nika Kahpho." Spaal, cumtux hyou kliminawhit wawau, "halo mesika memaloost Chee-Chee-Ka, yaka hyas klosh kopa nesika, yaka kwansum wawau kentsum, mash killipi, pe nesika iskum lakwitchee, pe chetlo-pe toluko.

Alta Il'kope yaka opoots, pe mahsh yaka; tillicum wawau, klosh, klosh. Pe yaka te'kope yaka opoots, pe hyou hee-hee pe potlatch okook opoots kopa tenas. Yaka kow Chee-Chee-Ka opoots kopa klosh kwek pe yaka staadi.

Konaway stikya tenas coolee pe hee-hee pe pok takwatz opoots. Chee-Chee-Ka hyou cli pe coolee kopa yaka chith, wawau, "Nanitch, nika opoots yaka tsolo ; klosh nika hyou tikegh pos mika temanous yaka iskum copa nika."

Klosh Chitsh wawau. Chitsh mamook hyou temanous, pe moxt yaka klatawa kopa scholtz, pe nanitch opoots. Konaway tenas mamook poh yaka. Pe Chitsh wawau, "Seewin hyak chahko okook opoots kopa Chee-Chee-Ka." Pe opoots staadi chahko kopa Chee-Chee-Ka, yaka hyak iskum hyou chumouck pos chummult yaka opoots pe halo kahta mamook. Yaka hyou snais Chee-Chee-Ka hyou sollecks pe mash yaka opoots klatlum, pe hyou sick tumtum. Yaka hyou shem, pe klatawa klawhap kopa smand, pe yaka kwass, pe kwansum ipoots halo chahko, til-til.

I now give the translation of the above story :

CHEE-CHE-KA.

Chee-che-ka was once upon a time a man who could change himself into mink shape. One day he had set his trap in the river and was watching the stick that held the door open. Presently the stick moved, and he let down the door and pulled up the trap. Instead of fish he caught a fine young wolf.

"Now, then, what are you doing in my trap?"

"Oh, I was looking for salmon trout. Please let me go."

"No, indeed; you have been stealing from me long enough, and now I will punish you."

So the poor wolf was killed, the fur and head taken off and stuffed.

By and bye the wolf's father came down to the river and asked Chee-che-ka if he had seen his son pass that way.

"No, I have not," answered Chee-che-ka, telling a lie. So the wolf asked all his friends, the bears, deer, sea lions, panthers—everyone he asked, and all the birds. But no one knew where his son was. He asked the blue-jay to find the child, so this boaster said: "Oh, yes, I will try, but it will be hard." So off he flew to look.

Then Chee-che-ka came forward and said: "Perhaps I can find your son."

"Very well," said the wolf; "if you bring him to me alive, I will be your slave."

So Chee-che-ka began to sing with his sisters, the snakes and mice. They beat the sticks and sang, and he called his spirits to help. He told his sisters to go all about the grass and woods, and to pretend to find the young wolf. Then they came back, empty-handed, and then he, with a great show of noise, brought out the head and skin, stuffed, of the poor young wolf.

"Here is your son, Stikya."

Then the crying and mourning began, and some of the animals made a dash to catch Chee-che-ka, but

 HAVE YOU HERE THE FIRE?
CHEE-CHE-KA.

he had turned into a mink and disappeared down a mouse-hole and ran along their roads and came up outside.   Just then the land-otter caught him, and the animals all came to hold a court and try him for killing their friend's son.   After much talking, the panther said in the court:

"Chee-che-ka must die.   He has killed our young friend, so must give up his life."

The death sentence was pronounced, but the coon and the raven begged to be heard.   The coon said.

"Don't kill him, for he is my friend."

The raven, who is a great lawyer and knows well how to tell lies, said :

"Don't kill him, for he is useful to us;   when we go digging clams, oysters and mussels, he orders the tide to keep away, so that it is dry for us to walk on. If you kill him there will be no one left to order the tide water back.   If you must punish him, cut off his tail.   So, after much considering, they agreed to cut off his tail.   So the tail was cut off and tied like a hoop, and given to the children to roll about. What fun they all had out of the tail !   Poor Chee-che-ka ran away to his grandmother and asked her to see if she could not get back his tail.   So she called her spirits and told them what she wished.   So off she and her grandson went to the place where they were shooting arrows at the hoop.   The spirits rolled the hoop to them, and Chee-che-ka seized it and ran off with it to try to stick it on again.   He put pitch on the end and stuck it on;   but he was so fat that the tail would not stick on, so he threw it away in great disgust.   He ran off to the woods and mountains, ashamed to show himself any more to people.

He has since then lost the power of becoming a man, and remains a mink.

CHILTSOP, OR FIRE STICK.

Chee-che-ka, before he became a mink, wished to know how to make fire.   Indeed, he knew many wonderful things and could do marvels, but the art of fire-making was unknown to him.   He was quite unhappy about it.   This fire was a wonderful thing; they could use it to cook with, and so he became so keen to find out that he and his brother went in search of the " chiltsop."   They left their grandmother at home to take care of the house, and took their bows and arrows with them in the canoe.   As they came to the different villages they asked if they had the chiltsop.   Some of the people never heard of it, so they promised the people that if they were successful in their search they would show them this new chiltsop.

After many months of wanderings they were almost in despair; and by chance they asked the raven if he could tell them where he could find this precious fire.

" Oh, yes," said he.   " My friends that came from the South this year told me that this fire was in a village far to the South.   Now, you must go straight this way " (pointing to the South).

So, thanking the raven, they went off; and after many moons they got to the village where the fire was. It was held sacred, and guarded in the chief's house. Being strangers, they were shown all manner of civility, and slept during the night in the chief's house. Then they asked to see how this wonderful fire was made. This was refused, so they thought they would have to steal some fire. The big stones round the fire were too hot and too large to carry away.

"I have a plan," said Chee-che-ka. "To-night, when they are all asleep, I'll steal the chief's child, and we'll run away. Then they will come after us, but I shall not give up the child till they tell us how they make fire."

Now, the cradle was hung on a stick, which was placed in a slanting position, and when the child was tied in the cradle, it rocked to sleep by swaying the stick from side to side gently. These cradles are very quaint, and are sometimes beautifully worked with colored porcupine quills, grass and feathers. The babies are tied in securely, so that they can be safely carried on their mothers' backs, or hung on a branch while she gathers roots and herbs.

Now, when all was quiet and the chief and his wife fast asleep, Chee-che-ka rose up and unhooked the cradle, and with his brother stole out of the lodge. The dogs knew them and did not bark, so off they started to the beach and jumped in their canoe and went off. As they passed the villages they would pirch the child so as to make it cry, and so on till they reached home. Now, the next morning when the poor mother awoke to feed her baby, she could not find it. She hunted everywhere for it, and at last awoke her husband. Then he knew that the strangers must have stolen his child. What misery and sorrow reigned in the village ! They tracked Chee-che-ka to the beach and found that his canoe was gone, so they got ready to follow him. The chief took many things to exchange for the child, such as copper and furs, and he took two precious fire-sticks with him, and he and his friends started. They asked all the people whose villages they passed if they had seen the child.

" No, we have seen no child, but we heard one crying as a canoe passed," and so on till they reached Chee-che-ka's house. They asked if she had seen the child, and she said yes, she had.

" Please let me have the child. I will give you all this canoe-load."

So she went back to the house to tell Chee-che-ka, but he refused the bribes. " Tell them I want the fire-sticks and then they can have the child."

So out she came and rubbed her hands together and made a strange little noise, like this : Close your teeth and strike them rapidly with your tongue, and you will hear the call she made. " Te-te-te!"—you must also sing one note, so as to make the quaint sound. Well, they understood what was wanted, and the chief came ashore and showed her how to make the chilsop and how to keep the fire alight. The babe was restored to its happy father, and all were pleased.

CHILDREN OF THE MOON.

Many years ago an Indian chief, living on the West Coast, was one day walking along the beach, looking for a suitable tree to make into a canoe. He saw, lying, a small round log, with one end smaller than the other and without any bark on, and quite smooth ; round the middle was a hard black substance. He examined it closely and found that this piece of black stuff could be taken off this smooth log, so he went to work and succeeded in loosening it, and at length it lay in his hand. Could he use this hard stuff to cut with ? He took a large stone and began to hammer away at this thing, and at last he broke it and flattened it out straight. Then he tried to cut wood with it, and found that he could easily drive the black thing into the wood. Overjoyed with his discovery, he tied a handle to this wonderful thing and called it his power. He told none of his friends about his discovery. He then began to make a canoe, and when it was finished, the inside and out were so smooth that his friends inquired of him how he had made such an improvement. He only laughed and said that the spirits had given him a great power. So his friends asked to be allowed to see this wonder; but he refused to show it to them. They kept a close watch on him, but could not find out what it was he used. So at last they left him alone. One day, whilst out hunting, he lost his power, and was inconsolable. He was afraid to ask his friends to help him look for his power, lest they might find it and keep it.

   'TIS THE MOON SHIP!

This great loss preyed upon his mind so much that he lost heart in everything; even his appetite had gone, and he decided that it was better to die than to live. So, climbing the righ mountain at the back of the village, and then on down the valley to a very high mountain he saw in the distance, he reached the top just as the moon was rising over the sea. What was his amazement to see the moon carrying on her breast a beautiful canoe, but larger than he had ever seen or dreamt of, and it had large white wings, spread out like a bird's. "Ah! It must be the children of the moon that have come down to earth. What is going to happen? Perhaps we are going to die, or our enemies are coming to attack us."

He watched this marvellous sight, and saw the moon's canoe glide away and out of sight. He was so full of fear and astonishment that he forgot completely that he had come up the mountain to die a lonely death. So eager was he to tell his people what he had seen that he rushed down the mountain side, leaping from stone to stone, like a young deer, and reached the village, breathless. He told them that he had seen the moon's canoe ; but the people laughed at the wonderful tale, and said that he had dreamed it, and his spirits were deceiving him.

Early next day, when they awoke, what should they see, lying in their harbour, but this wonderful canoe that the chief had seen.

"Now, then, did I not tell you the truth? Here, this canoe has come to visit us. Come, let us go and see the moon's children."

They were afraid, and called a council meeting to decide what had better be done. So, after much talking, they decided to send twelve young men, who were pure in heart and body, to go and visit the moon's canoe. So a large war canoe was got ready, and these twelve youths stepped in. As they were pushing off, our friend jumped in. His curiosity was so great he could not resist the temptation of being one of the first to see these wonderful things. They paddled round this big canoe. It was so high and long! How could they get on it? So the moon children let down pieces of stuff, like cedar bark rope, and made signs for them to catch hold of these ropes and come up. They did so, and when they reached the deck, the chief of the moon children came to meet them. He had a very white face and eyes like the blue skies, and hair like grass when it is yellow. He made signs to them not to be afraid, and made them sit down, and placed before them bright, shining dishes, filled with blood and bones, and made signs for them to eat. They shook their heads and talked among themselves, asking, how could they eat such stuff as blood and bones. Then one of the moon children took a piece of bone and thrust it into the blood and put it into his mouth and eat it. One of the young men took heart and followed his example. How good it was! He told his companions to eat it, for, he said, " It is sweet, just like our mother's milk." So they fell to and enjoyed it, as they had never done anything before.

After they had finished, the moon's people came and felt their dresses, which were made of sea-otter furs. The people seemed to like the feel of their clothes so much that one of the young men suggested that they make them a present of their furs. So the young men took off their clothes and laid them down on the deck, and made signs that they meant the skins as a gift for the wonderful men.   Now the men took long sticks, and, pointing at a flock of ducks flying overhead, a loud noise was made, and smoke came pouring out of the fire-stick.   The poor fellows fell down and were almost beside themselves with fear. The men then picked up a duck that had fallen on the deck, and showed it to them.   The young men were struck with wonderment, and made signs that they wished to have a fire-stick.   The moon people made signs that they would give the fire-stick for furs, so some of the young men went ashore and told these things, and they were laden with bales of sea-otter skins, which they took to the ship, and laid down by the fire-stick, which was held up as a measure.   Then they were given the fire-stick and shown how to handle it, and great was their satisfaction.

"Now we have something better than our bows and arrows, and can kill all the bears we need."

The chief was given the moon dishes, which he hung up afterwards in his lodge.   How brightly they shone, and were just as round as the moon.

This was the first time that they had seen white men, or tasted molasses and biscuit, or handled a gun, or seen a tin dish.

FOLK LORE OF THE CREE INDIANS.

As a little girl I used to listen to these legends with the greatest delight, and in order not to lose them, I have written down what I can remember of them. When written they lose their charm which was in the telling. They need the quaint songs and the sweet voice that told them, the winter gloaming and the bright fire as the only light—then were these legends beautiful.

MARTHA DOUGLAS HARRIS.

WIE-SAH-KE-CHACK.

In olden days a great flood came upon earth, and all the people were destroyed except Wie-sah-ke-chack and a few animals. They were on a raft. It was terrible. After a long time of it, Wie-sah-ke-chack said to the animals: " Which of you will go down and see if you can find the earth. Bring me a little and I will make a new world."

The little water-rat tried, but he could not go far enough down; so the beaver offered to go; and, after tying a long string to one of his feet, he sprang off the raft and down into the water. The string quivered, and at last stopped. "Our brother is dead." So they pulled up the beaver, and sure enough he was dead, but in his paws he held a little earth. This Wie-sah-ke-chack took and, blowing into the beaver's face, he came to life again. Then Wie-sah-ke-chack made a small ball of the earth, and kept blowing on it, and it grew larger and larger, till it was so large that he thought it was large enough for them to live on, so he asked the wolf to go and see ; but the wolf came back and said that it was not half large enough, so he kept blowing and the earth growing, and the second time the wolf went; but no, it was not large enough. The third time the wolf went to see, he never came back, so from that they knew that the world was big enough for all to live on. That is the beginning of the world. Many years after—I don't know how many, but long enough for the people to increase—Wie-sah-ke-chack was walking along one day singing his song—he always carried his song on his back—when he saw a man sitting on a log, taking out his eyes and throwing them up in the air. He stood and looked with astonishment at this wonderful thing. He then shewed himself and asked what his brother was doing.

"Oh," said the man, "my head was aching, and this is the way I cure myself."

"Oh, please show me, too."

"Remember," said the man, after shewing Wie-sah-ke-chack how to do the trick, "only do it when your head really aches ; if you do it when it does not, you will lose your eyes."

He promised faithfully, so they parted, and Wie-sah-ke-chack was all impatience to try the new remedy. At last he got a headache and then joy; he could throw his eyes up in the air. " How much better I feel now," said he, after playing a long time with his eyes. Then he went on his journey again, but still longing to try again. At last he could not resist the temptation, and, sitting down, exclaimed: "What a headache I have; how ill I feel!"—all make believe. So out came his eyes, and for several times they dropped into the sockets safely. At last they fell on the ground and were snapped up by a white fox, who had been watching him. How Wie-sah-ke-chack cried and lamented the loss of his eyes, when suddenly he felt a sharp prick on his poor empty eye-sockets. " Who is trying to hurt me, now that I have lost my eyes ? If I catch him I will kill him."

Then the pricking still went on, till he was perfectly frantic. At last he caught the white fox by his leg and held him up and threatened to pull him to pieces. The fox prayed him to let him go, " for," said the fox, " I will take you to a place where you can get some pitch and make eyes for yourself."

Wie-sah-ke-chack would not let the fox go, but tied him with a cord, so the fox led him to an old pine tree, and there he found good white pitch and made eyes for himself ; but his eye-lids were always red, and that is the reason why old people get red eyes from Wie-sah-ke-chack.

After his eyes were restored, he went on and saw a beaver lying asleep, and he ran and caught him by the tail, and put his fire-bag on a tree-limb overhanging the water, and forgot it there. The beaver he tied to his back and went to make a fire and cook the beaver. Presently the beaver gave him such a slap with his tail, and then another, that Wie-sah-ke-chack was glad to let him go. "Now, where is my fire-bag?" So he went back to where he had found the beaver, and there, in the water, was the bag. How was he to get it? At last the beaver got there, and laughed at him. "Look up, you stupid, and see where it is; but you won't make a fire for me to-day."

So Wie-sah-ke-chack had to go hungry. He pulled in his belt. He was so famished, and he was walking on very sadly when he came across a beautiful deer. " Now, here is my meat." Then, calling to the deer, he said: " Good day, brother; let us play a while, and do you pretend I am going to shoot you, but I'll only pretend."

So the deer began to run up and down, tossing his beautiful head and springing in the air; the arrows would fall short, and Wie-sah-ke-chack would pretend to be vexed. At last he aimed at the deer's heart and shot at his poor brother and killed him. Now what a feast he would have! So, skinning the deer and getting the fire ready and cutting the choicest bits and putting them on la pola sticks to broil before the fire, he did not know if he had better sleep first or wash first, so he said he would sleep after the feast. So he went to the water-side, and, bathing himself carefully and combing his hair, at length he was ready, and how good the meat smelt! So, going to two pine trees that were growing out of one stem, he got between them and told them to squeeze him till his appetite was better. The trees began to squeeze him gently, but firmly. Now, this good smell of cooking had brought all the animals to the feast, and they began, without ceremony, to eat the feast. " Stop! Stop! That is my feast. Here, let me go!"

but the trees held him fast, and in his anger he broke all the branches he could reach and threw them at the animals. At last everything was eaten, and the bones picked clean, and the fire put out, and the uninvited guests dispersed, when the trees let him loose. These trees are called Wie-sah-ke-chack trees, as they punished him for his greediness. Now he fumed and raged, but to no purpose. Going along, he found a man who was hunting, but this hunting was new to Wie-sah-ke-chack. The man had a number of little men who hunted for him, and they had killed a large deer. He opened a large sack and called the little men to come back, and they all stepped into the sack, and he shut it up. Now, Wie-sah-ke-chack stepped out and said: " Good day, brother. What are you doing here ? "

" Oh, I am just hunting."

" And what have you in your bag ? "

" I have my little men, and they hunt for me."

" Oh, how I wish I could have some hunters, too."

" Well," said the stranger, " I'll be glad to give you some; but when you are hunting, don't let the little men go out of sight, or you will lose them." So, giving Wie-sah-ke-chack some men and picking up the deer, the stranger disappeared.

How happy was our friend, and he strode off into the woods, quite happy. Presently he came into a large open glade, and there he saw a deer grazing, so opening the sack, he let the little men out, and they ran and shot the deer. He was so busy with the deer that he forgot to call the little men back, and they disappeared, and he was inconsolable. So he cooked his deer and ate it; and the next day, shouldering his sack, off he went.

The birds had all assembled before winter. They had called a meeting, and after the meeting they were to have a dance ; but there was no one to sing for them, when suddenly they saw Wie-sah-ke-chack coming. What calling and shouting ! " Come here, Wie-sah-ke-chack; how glad we are to see you, for we are going to have a big dance to-night, and we want you to sing for us."

" Hey!" cried he; " why, you have nothing ready for your dance."

" Well, what must we do ? "

" First of all," said he, " you must build a big lodge, and put a division in the middle of it, and by and by the fat birds must dance on one side and the lean ones on the other, and then I must paint you."

So they were all busy, and after the lodge was made, they came to be painted. Out of the sack the paints came, and the swan was the first to get ready; so Wie-sah-ke-chack painted him all white, with black feet and nose. How beautiful he looked. Then the wood-duck, with all his lovely colours on. It was a rare sight to see these painted birds. Well, when they were all ready the fat birds went to one side and the lean to the other, and then they were told to shut their eyes while they danced. Such fine songs Wie-sah-ke-chack sung! I have forgotten them now, so I can't tell you how they went. By and by the noise of the dancing became less and less, and at last La Pcoldo, the little water-hen, opened her eyes—and what should she see but Wie-sah-ke-chack killing her people and throwing them outside—only the fat ones. of course. So she got near the door and then shouted, "Wie-sah-ke-chack is killing us!" and as she ran out of the door he stepped on her back and almost broke it, and that is why the water-hen is now so clumsy when she walks. Then the dance broke up, and the birds that were left flew away. Now, there was a fine beach there—a long stretch of lovely white sand—and Wie-sah-ke-chack thought he would make his feast there, so he buried the birds, with their legs sticking up, and built a big fire over them. Then he lay down and slept, and when he awakened he went to bathe and refresh himself. What a fine appetite he had, and how he would enjoy himself after all the hard work! So, scraping the ashes away, he pulled up the first bird, and only legs came up—no body at all. Well, the fire must have been too hot. Then he tried the next bird, and the same thing happened; so he ran along, pulling up his feast, but nothing but legs came. Then he knew his feast had been stolen from him. It seems that the foxes had come down and eaten all the birds up whilst he slept, and then stuck the legs back again so as to deceive Wie-sah-ke-chack.

There are other adventures, but they are not clear in my mind, so I will not write them. The legend is that the person who can tell all about the adventures of Wie-sah-ke-chack will live to be very old. So I leave my story, with great reluctance, owing to my inability to remember more, and having to face a short life in consequence.

These stories lose so much in the writing.

THE STORY OF THE FOUR WINDS.

In a village by the river there lived a very hand-some young man, who was content to live with his sister and employ his time hunting. His sister was very industrious, and put up many things for the long winters. She was very plain, and no one cared to marry her, though she was known to be so good and clever. One day she said to her brother: "My brother, you must now think of getting a wife. The girls are all dying of jealousy when you go to see them. Now, please choose one and bring her home."

"Well, sister, you ask me a hard thing to do, for I don't like any of them ; but if you say I must marry, well I have to obey you. Now, when they come to see me in the lodge, the one that is able to hang my blanket on the sunbeam and then see me— for I shall be invisible to everyone except you—I will marry."

"Well, you have given them a hard task, but I will call the girls to-morrow."

So he went to invite all the girls to come to see her brother, who, she said, was going to choose a wife. What excitement reigned ! The next day early the pretty girls went in, one by one. "Take this blanket, sister, and hang it on this sunbeam."

The girl tried her best, but it was impossible to do it.

"Now, sister, do you see my brother ?"

The poor girl had to say no. Then all the girls were tried, but none could see him or put the blanket

(Copyrighted.)   A VERY HIDEOUS OLD WOMAN
SKILLED IN MAGIC.

on the sunbeam.   Now, there lived in the village a very hideous old woman, skilled in magic, and when she heard that the girls had all been refused, she was angry and went off to the young man's lodge.   When the sister saw her come in, she knew it was all up with her brother, but she said: " Good day, sister;   can you put the blanket on this sunbeam ? "

" Yes, indeed I can," so she immediately hung the blanket up.

" Now, sister, do you see my brother ? "

" Hey!   Of course I do; there he sits, dressed in a green coat made of ducks' necks, and a cap of the swans' breasts."

So the young man lamented his stupidity in refusing the pretty girls and having to marry this hateful old thing.   Marry he had to, but with very bad grace. The next day he went out hunting, and she went with him to bring home the meat, and when far away he turned on her and killed her and cut her to pieces and went home.   The next day he went out again, and who should he see but his wife coming towards him, singing to a child.   " See our child ! " she cried, and he had to go to her.   It seems that during the struggle he had lost some fringe off his coat, and out of this she made a child.   So he tried to kill her again; but after a long struggle she was the victor, but before he died: " Never let our daughter stoop down to the east when she goes to gather sticks for the fire." Then he died.   The old woman went back to the village with the child, and lived with the young man's sister. She never would tell what had happened to him.   She was very careful of the child, and as soon as she could run about, she told her never to stoop down to the east, where the sun rose from.   What would happen

she could not tell. One day, when the girl was about
sixteen, she went to gather wood, and forgot all about
the caution, when she stooped down towards the sun.
Then she was carried away and became the mother of
the four winds. They all have names, but I have forgotten them.

THE ENCHANTED BEAR.

In a very large village there lived two sisters.
They had lost their parents when the younger child
was but a babe and the eldest a child of about twelve
years of age. This good girl took entire charge of
her little sister, and also worked for the women of the
village, and they gave her food in return for her help.
When the little girl was old enough to play with the
other children, her sister begged her never to play the
game that the children were fondest of, and that was
calling out, " Bear ! Bear ! " and frightening themselves with pretending that they were being chased.
So the little girl was very careful to obey her sister,
as she loved her greatly; and when the game was to
be played, she would run back to her sister. At length
the children noticed it, and said: " Now, it is your
turn to be bear." She begged them not to ask her to
play it. Children are sometimes cruel, and they insisted on her taking her turn, so she had to submit or
be cruelly used. Well, she went into the hiding place,
and when the children shouted "Bear! Bear!" out she
came, growling at them, and chased them and then

ran home to tell her sister what she had been compelled to do. There, owing to this unfortunate game, when she reached home she found that her poor sister had been transformed into a bear. The poor bear was crying at this horrid change, and asked her sister to go with her to the river side and live in a cave in the bank. They both wept together, and then they went to find this cave and make it their home. Then the people heard of the sister being changed into a bear, and came and mocked the little sister, and out rushed the bear and destroyed many of the people. The rest got very much alarmed, and tried in many ways to kill the bear, but all their efforts were in vain. At last they tried making a fire before the cave's mouth, but she only rushed out and attacked them. They could not kill this enchanted bear. They waylaid the poor sister and asked her where the bear kept her heart.

"Oh, I don't know; indeed I don't," she would say. At last they insisted on her asking the bear where her heart was. So one evening she began asking questions, and at last came to ask where the bear's heart was kept. "Now, my sister, the people have told you to ask me."

"No, sister, they have not."

At last she told where her heart was. It was in her forepaw, in the little toe of it. So the next day when the little sister went to draw water, she was waylaid and compelled to tell where the bear's heart was.

For many days the men were very busy making little sticks, pointed at both ends, and when they had finished they went towards the bear's cave, and stuck these sharp points into the ground, as closely together as they could. Then they shouted to the bear to come out, and roused the bear at once, who came rushing out, right on these sharp sticks. One pricked her little toe, and she fell dead, to the bitter grief of her younger sister.

CHIS-TAPISTAQUHN, OR THE ROLLING HEAD.

A man, his wife and two little sons went into the forest to hunt and fish, so as to get sufficient food for the winter, the winter being very long and cold. The father was very fortunate in his hunting. Many moose had he killed, also ducks and geese in plenty; he had trapped plenty of beaver, otter and marten; their furs were for clothing.   His wife, however, was a very lazy woman, and let much of the meat spoil. One day he asked his little children: "What does your mother do when I am away ?"

"Oh, father, she leaves us and will not let us follow her.   She goes far away, and does not come back till it is nearly time for you to come home."

The father was very sad, and could not rest till he found out what his wife did during his absence. So the next morning he went off to see his traps, etc., but only went a little way, and then waited for his wife.

Presently she came out, dressed in her best, and went towards the river.   He followed her, and saw her stop at a very large stump and knock at it and say: "I am here my friends; come out now and let us play."

Then the stump became alive with snakes, large

and small. Then she laid down and let them crawl all over her, and kept singing and playing with them. The poor man was almost overcome with terror, but tore himself away and made his plan how he was going to destroy this monster of a woman. So he shot many deer and left them and marked the places where they were hid, and went home. He had killed some beaver and had taken their teeth with him, but left them in the swamps. In the evening he told his wife that she must get up early next day and go into the woods and bring back the meat and beaver. How cross she was! She scolded her children and behaved quite rudely. Next day she went off, and not long afterwards he went to find the stump, and when he found it he took a stick and beat on it and said: " Come out, my friends; I am here now; come and play."

Then the snakes all came out, and he began cutting them to pieces. He killed all of them except one little snake that managed to escape into its hole. He gathered all the blood of the snakes and took it home. At dusk the wife returned, very tired and cross. He had cooked the beavers' tails, which are most delicious and a great dainty, and afterwards gave her to drink, but it was blood. She did not know it. He had told his children that he had killed their mother's friends, and that when she found out she would kill them all. " Now, listen, my children. You must run away from here as quickly as you can; and if you see your mother coming after you, you must throw this comb behind you." Then he gave them a wooden comb, flint and beaver's teeth. " Always remember and throw these things behind you and never in front." Then he lifted up the flap of the skin tent at the back, and told them to go that way.   The poor little fellows went off crying bitterly.

Now, the mother, after eating and feeling better, asked where the children were.

" Oh, they are watching for the stars, and will be in soon, so go to sleep.   The next day he left early, but went only a little way, when he saw his wife go out.   Presently she came back, raging.   She had gone to the stump and found all her friends dead, and only one little one left alive, who told her that her husband had killed all his relations.   When he heard her raging he returned and prepared for the death struggle.   Words cannot describe the awful conflict. At last he cut off her head and fled, with the body after him and the head rolling about looking for the children, and calling for them.   At last she saw a crow, and asked the bird if he had seen which way the children had gone.

" Oh, yes," said he; " lift up the tent at the back and you will find their trail."

So he flew down and picked up the tent, and out the head rolled.   It went on and on till it nearly reached the children, who were terribly frightened. They threw the comb behind, and an immense forest sprang up.   Now the head was in despair, and asked everybody she met to help her. At last the fire helped her and made a path for her through the forest.   She then rolled on and nearly came up to the children, when they threw the flint, and a great mountain rose up.   Again she asked the birds and animals to help her.   An eagle picked her up and carried her over and dropped her, and she went rolling on.

At last the poor children saw her coming, and in their haste they threw the beaver's teeth before them, and a broad river appeared.   Poor children, how could they cross this wide river? They cried so bitterly that at last a pelican that was fishing near by, said: " Come, my poor little children; get on my back and I will cross you."

" Oh, grandfather, how kind you are."

On the broad back of the pelican they mounted, and he took them across the river. The head saw the children get on the pelican's back, but was too late to catch them. So when the pelican came back, she begged him to cross her too. At first he would not, but at last consented, and after a good deal of trouble she got on the pelican's back. Just when they were in the middle of the river he made a dive after a fish, and the poor Chis-tapistaquhn rolled into the water, where she became a sturgeon. The Indians won't eat the flesh of the sturgeon just where the head joins the body, for that is, they say, Chis-tapistaquhn's flesh. The poor children remained on the river bank, living as best they could, when one day a temanhous man came and carried away the eldest boy for his daughter's husband. The poor little boy was heart-broken at parting with his brother, but the temanhous man turned the younger into a wolf.

THE TWO SISTERS.

In the days of old, when the stars came down on earth and talked with men, two young girls lived. The eldest was a silly girl and a regular torment to her younger sister, who was her opposite in everything.   One summer evening they went down to the riverside, and, after bathing, lay down under a large tree and talked about many things.   At last they spoke about the stars, and the elder began to say how she would like to marry that big shining star, and in fun the younger one chose the smallest star.   Well, they fell asleep, and by and by awoke to find that the stars had come down as their husbands.   The big star was a very old red-eyed man, but the small star was young and handsome.   So they were carried up to the sky, and the younger sister was very happy.   The elder sister, however, was very miserable, and kept teasing her sister to find a way to escape.   At last, after a great deal of trouble, the younger sister consented to leave her star husband ;   so off they went to find some way of getting back to earth.   They found a wise woman, who gave them a large basket, and, after tying them in and cautioning them not to open their eyes when she let them down to earth, she bound their eyes, and, taking a long rope, opened a door in the sky and let them down.   Now, the eldest sister, whose great fault was curiosity, wished to know why they were not to look as they were going down.   Her sister begged her to keep quiet, or they might get into trouble.   She, however, insisted on seeing where they were going.   As she looked they struck a tall tree, and there the basket stuck.

"Now, just see what you have done, you stupid girl.   How are we going to get down ? "

They could not move.   They called to the animals that passed below, " Come and help us get down." They all refused but the carcajou.   Before he came up he wanted them to promise that they would marry him. After a long time they consented to the proposition. He clambered up the tree and wished to take the younger sister down first.

"Oh, no ; you must take my eldest sister, or I won't marry you." So he was forced to take the elder down first. Then the young sister took her hair-string and wound it round and round the tree, and knotted it many times. Then the carcajou came to take her down. So they went on to his lodge, but before they reached the place the younger sister exclaimed that she had lost her hair-string, and that she must have it.

"Where did you lose it ? "

"How do I know ? Please go and look for it."

Carcajou went to look for it, and after a long hunt he found it tied at the top of the tree. In the meantime the two sisters ran as quickly as they could, so as to escape from the carcajou, or wolverine. Towards evening they sat down to rest, and they heard a baby crying in the woods.

"Hist! There is a child crying," said the elder. "I must go and find it."

"No, no, please don't go ; perhaps it is only a trick of Carcajou."

But this silly girl went off to look for the child. In a little while she came back with a child tied in a beautiful cradle, and she sang to it and kissed it, and made a great to do over it, when all at once she saw it change to Carcajou, who laughed heartily at them for trying to run away from him.

"So you thought you could deceive me, but I tell you that I can turn myself into anything, and you can't escape me. Here, take your hair-string, and get my supper ready."

    She Came Back with a Child Tied
in a Cradle.

"The sisters went to work cooking the supper, and the younger one put in some roots that caused sleep. The carcajou liked his supper, and then rolled off into a deep sleep.

"Come, sister, let us be quick, for he will sleep for a very long time, and let us run away."

How fast they ran, scarcely stopping to take breath. At last they came to a large river. Now, how could they cross? They called to the fish to come and help them, but they all refused. Just then a large drake flew down and swam towards them, and asked them what they wanted.

"Oh, brother, would you be so kind as to take us across the river?"

"Well, I don't know; what will you give me? Will you marry me."

They promised to be his wives. Then he crossed first one and then the other—he carried them on his back. He took them to his favourite swamp, and there gave them roots to eat.

"Now, this evening I am going to a big dance, but I won't be away long, so keep up the fire and go to sleep."

They promised faithfully. Then he bathed himself and plumed each feather till he shone, and put his song on his back, and off he flew.

Then the young sister hunted for two rotten logs, so she might dress them as women. At last she found what she wanted, and dressed them, and lay them down, and off they ran. By and by the drake came home and snuggled down between his wives. First one would pinch him, and then the other, and so on, till he woke. "Stop pinching me, I say!" Then he would sleep, but at last the pinching became so hard that he awoke, and found that instead of women he was lying between logs, just full of ants. The women escaped and got home safely.

THE ADVENTURES OF HYAS.

Once upon a time, in days when much magic was the fashion, there lived a man who dealt in evil spirits, but he was a very plausible, smooth-speaking old person. He had two wives; The first wife was now old, and had to do slave's work for the second, who had everything her own way. The first wife had an only son; Hyas was his name, and she had prayed the good spirits of her tribe to bless and care for her darling. When the lad was about twelve years old, he was out in the woods one day and spied a partridge nest full of young birds; he took it home with him for his small step-brothers and sisters to play with. When he reached home, he happened to meet his father's second wife at the door, who said:

"What have you got there, Hyas?"

"Oh, nothing," said he.

"Let me see," and she snatched the nest and birds out of his hands, and the little things flew in her face and scratched her. Then she began to call Hyas names.

"Well, you would see the partridges, and I brought them home for the children to play with."

"Never mind; I'll tell your father what you have done to me."

At evening the father came back from his hunting, so tired, and the young wife shewed her face and said: "See how your son, that hateful Hyas, has scratched my face."

The old man was very angry, and said: "Stop ! Stop ! To-morrow I'll pay him for this ; keep quiet and you'll see what will happen."

Early next morning the old man called Hyas and said : "My dear son, yesterday I found a nest with red eggs in it, and I left them there, thinking you would like to get them yourself."

"Where ? Where ?" cried Hyas, much excited. "I have always wished to find red eggs. How glad I am that I shall at last see them."

"Well," said his father, come with me and I'll show you."

So into the canoe they got and off they went, Hyas first kissing his mother, but she wept, she was so sad, for she feared some evil would befall her son. For Hyas was her only stand-by, and he would never let the young wife ill-treat her. However, he would be home in the evening.

Now, the canoe was a magic one, and all one had to do was to strike it and off it would shoot along the water, and when it slackened—whack! give it another blow, and that was all that was needed. At last, near evening, they came to an island, right in the centre of the wide river. "Now, my son," said the father, "jump ashore ; this is the island where I found the red eggs."

"Thank you, my father; I will not be long," and Hyas bounded off, so anxious to secure this great prize. Just as soon as Hyas had disappeared, the old man turned his canoe homeward, and left his voice

(Copyrighted.) OH! MY FATHER, DO NOT LEAVE ME HERE
TO DIE. COME BACK FOR ME!

behind to speak to Hyas and lure him further into the woods. Whack! and the canoe sped away, leaving poor Hyas. Hyas hunted, hunted everywhere, then cried to his father: " I can't find the red ones."

" Go into the middle of the island ; there you will find them," answered the voice.

So at it again, up and down through the little island, searched Hyas; but how could he find the eggs, as there were none there to find ? So, in despair, he at last came back to the water's edge. Ah! but where was the canoe ? Hyas looked and saw it far out on the stream, going ever further away from the shore. " Father! Father! Come back and take me home."

" No, indeed, not after you scratched my wife's face."

" No, no; I did not. She would play with the young partridges, and they scratched her."

" Well, stay where you are and die ; I am tired of supporting you," and swiftly the canoe carried the evil old man far away—far away home.

Hyas threw himself down, crying. He could not swim that swift river. He had not tools to make a canoe with, so he gave himself up to despair.

Hist ! A voice ! " Hyas, get up; don't cry, and shoot one of the gulls that are flying about."

At first Hyas would not move, but the voice kept calling: " Hyas, Hyas, take the gull's skin, and you can fly across the river." So at last he was persuaded, and, taking his small bow and arrows, he got up and started to shoot at the gulls. At last he killed one— a young bird—and skinned it, put it on and began to fly. He circled near the shore, but alas! it burst, and down fell poor Hyas. How he cried, but the voice urged him again. "Hyas! Hyas! Shoot an old bird—a white one." So again the poor lad tried and managed to shoot a very large one. So with great haste he skinned it and put it round his body and began to fly—this time across the river. When near the opposite shore the skin burst and he fell into the water, but was just able to swim to shore. He thanked the spirit for helping him, and off he went. "Chee! Chee!" he heard a voice calling, and, looking up, he saw an old squirrel, who said: "Is that you, my grandson? I heard that your father had left you on the island to die. How bitterly I have cried. You see my eyes are quite red with weeping."

"Yes, grandmother, my father is a wicked man. Now, tell me how I may get home."

"Come first and eat," said the squirrel, and she laid a large store of nuts and roots before poor Hyas. "The way is very long and full of your father's evil spirits, my grandson. You must try and kill these, and then you will get home. Take these shoes with you, and when in danger put them on, and you will be able to escape."

She gave him a beautiful little pair of squirrel magic shoes, so that if he wished to escape from danger all he had to do was to put them on and he would turn to a squirrel. He thanked her and went off.

The next day he met a huge toad, who was waiting for him. This was one of his father's evil spirits. "Good day, my grandson; where are you going?" she croaked.

"I am going home," said he.

"The way is very dangerous, and I would help you; so take these shoes, and when you are in danger put them on, and you can become like me." If he had once put on her shoes, he would have remained a toad.

"Tish!" said Hyas, scornfully, and stamped on the toad and crushed her flat. Walking on he came to a wide river. Now, how was he to get over ? He did not know, so he must get some one to tell him. Just then a little green frog appeared and said: "Hie! Is that you, Hyas ?"

"Yes, I am Hyas."

"I have been looking for you, for I heard that your father had left you on the island, and that you had got off. Now, I will help you. When you are in danger, use these little shoes I give you, and you will become like me."

"Thank you, grandmother ; but how am I to cross this river ?"

"Well, we must ask your grandfather, the great snake, what he can do ; he is very old now. Come, let us find him." So they went down to the edge of the river, and there, on the beach, they found a monster snake lying; and, after much calling and poking with a stick to make him awake, he raised his head and asked why they disturbed him.

"It is Hyas, who wishes to cross," said the little frog.

"If it is Hyas, then, I will help him. See first, Hyas, if there are any clouds in the sky."

When Hyas said that the sky was clear, he said: "Now, put my head in the water and get on my back and tell me how to go, for I am very blind; and if I slacken speed, strike my horns."

So Hyas put the snake in the water and jumped on his back, and struck the snake's horns. It sounded just like thunder. Now, Hyas had noticed a tiny black cloud in the sky when the snake asked if there were any ; but, thinking that so small a cloud was of no importance, he had said nothing about it. While the two were half across, the tiny cloud increased till it filled the sky, and then the thunder and lightning began to dance the storm dance. "What is that, my son ? Is it thunder I hear ? I am so deaf."

"No, no, grandfather ; it is just the sound that I make when I strike your horns."

When near the shore, suddenly the lightning and thunder struck the poor old snake and killed him. Hyas jumped ashore, weeping, because it was his fault the poor grandfather was killed. Weeping, Hyas gathered in some cedar bark the blood of the poor old snake and lay down beside it to sleep. By and by he heard scratching inside the bark, and when he moved it, there lay a young snake. He was so pleased, and put the snake in the water and it swam away. So on Hyas went till he met a little white fox.

"Well, Hyas, so you have escaped. I am glad to see you. I am one of the spirits sent to show you your way."

"I thank you, fox."

"Now, you must do all I tell you. Not far from here lives one of your father's bad spirits ; he is a fair-speaking man, but will try to kill you. Before we reach his lodge, you must hide me in your coat, and don't eat anything he gives you, and don't sleep." So by and by they came near the place, and Hyas hid the little fox in his coat and went on; and, sure enough, there was a man sitting outside the lodge, who seemed so glad to see Hyas. "Come in, my dear

child, come in ; you must be so tired and hungry.
Come in, and I will shelter you for to-night."

So the man and Hyas went into the lodge, where
a fire was burning in the middle. Now, this man had
a very sore leg—how nasty it was I may not tell. He,
however, was very pleasant to Hyas, and when all was
ready he said : " Now, Hyas, come and eat." But
first of all he had squeezed his leg and put the poison
in the food. The fox whispered : " Make believe
that you are eating, and just drop the food down the
inside of your coat, and I will eat it." The man was
very lame, but also very pleasant. So Hyas pretended to eat, and said how delicious the food was,
while all the time giving it to the fox.

" Now, my son, you must be tired ; go yonder
and lie down on those skins, and I will tell you stories
till you go to sleep."

" Very well; I am tired, and I know I shall soon
sleep," said Hyas, and he lay down on the skins on his
side of the fire. Then the man commenced to tell
him his stories. Every now and then he would cry,
" Hyas, do you sleep ? " and Hyas would say, " Nay,
Hum ! " and the man, finding Hyas did not sleep,
would continue his story. At last the fox said :
" Don't answer him, but keep wide awake." The
usual question, " Do you sleep, Hyas ? " met with no
response ; but the man, to make sure, kept on with
the story till Hyas began to snore. Then he jumped
up, and, unbuckling his bad leg, was just going to
throw it on poor Hyas, when out bounded the fox,
who seized the leg and shook it violently. Hyas, too,
jumped up, and together they killed the man. How
grateful Hyas was to the white fox. " Now go, my
son, and be careful, for the next danger will be

greater. You will hear women laughing and singing, and they will ask you to play with them, but you must kill them, as they are your enemies." So saying he bid Hyas good speed and disappeared into the woods. Hyas trudged on, and the next day he heard great laughing. "Ha! Ha! Ha!" Peeping through the bushes he saw two women sitting in a high swing, and they laughed to think Hyas was coming, and how they should kill him. They had killed many people on this swing. Just below it was a large flat stone, and here they upset their victims. Then, with much fuss and noise, when Hyas shewed himself they rushed to him and desired to kiss him; but no, Hyas would not be kissed.

"Come, Hyas, just get into the swing and let us swing you."

"No, no," said he. "Let me swing you first. Both of you get in and I'll try."

So, laughing greatly, they both got in, and Hyas pushed and pushed, and pretended they were heavy. "Hu-uh! You are so heavy." All at once he put forth all his strength, and gave the swing a mighty push, and the two women went flying out and fell, crushing their heads on the flat stone below, on the place where many other victims had died. So those enemies were destroyed.

By the next day Hyas reached the place where the giants lived. They had a large dog, who took care of their hearts. He saw Hyas coming, and barked away like mad. "Hyas is coming—make ready for Hyas." Hyas then put on the shoes that his grandmother squirrel had given him, and when the giants came running out they saw nothing. So they scolded the dog, who still insisted Hyas was there. " Well," said one giant, " if you have seen him, to-morrow your eyes will be red."   So back they went to the lodge, and Hyas shewed himself again to the dog, who was barking furiously.   Now, the giants kept their hearts in an eagle's nest on the top of a tall pine tree, which the dog guarded. So the next day, when the giants came out there, truly, the dog had seen Hyas, for his eyes were very red. So they hunted and called for Hyas, up and down ; but he had turned himself into an eagle's down, and floated up, up to the top of the pine tree where the giants' hearts were kept.   Up, up, floated the down, then swiftly came down on one of the hearts and pierced it.   Down fell one of the giants with a loud groan, dead.   Then there was great trouble amongst them, but again Hyas flew up and came down with the sharp end of the feather on another heart, and another giant fell dead.   At last he had killed them all.   Then he took their store of good things and went on. ·

Now, the fox had told him of the dangers he would meet with, and how he should overcome all his enemies, so Hyas was well prepared.   The next trial now came.   Towards evening he saw a lodge, and, coming softly up, he perceived two blind old women sitting on either side of the door. They were talking about him and wondering when he would come.   " It is about time for him to arrive," said one sister.   So Hyas quietly slipped in between them and sat down inside.   Now, round the lodge they had bags and bags of marrow fat.   Hyas, going in, sat down by some of these bags. "Now," said one sister, " I'll go in and put the kettle on to boil, and if he comes the water will taste of marrow, and perhaps he will be here soon." So she went to work, and soon the water boiled, and Hyas stepped up and dropped in a sack of marrow. The old woman said : " Let me see if Hyas has come." She tasted the water and it tasted of marrow. " Hyas, are you here ? " No answer. " Hyas, are you here ? " Still no answer. Then she took a stick and began to poke about and count the bags; at last the stick struck Hyas. "Well, Hyas, so you have come. Welcome, welcome." And the two old wretches pretended to be so glad to see him, and gave him nice things to eat, and talked sweetly. At last he said he must go. Instantly they bared their arms, and out of their elbows were long bones, sharp as knives, and rushed to the door, to be ready to kill Hyas as he went out. He quick as thought took a bundle and put it on a stick and placed it between them. Then the fight began. Thinking they were hitting Hyas, the old wretches were striking each other, and soon they fell over, dead. How Hyas laughed. " Ho-o-ho ! " He went on his way rejoicing. Not long after he heard a great noise, and as he came out of the woods he saw a great plain. Stretched across the plain was a string, held up at the ends of the world, and on it were hung bones—oh, how many millions ! Deer bones, moose horns, elk, bison, goat—everything—jaw bones, thigh bones— too many to count. The bones would come down and strike the earth—crash!—and then would bound up into the air, and while the bones were in the air the earth would open her mouth, and no one could possibly cross. Oh, the din ! The horrid bones would drop down—crash!—all the time singing a wild song, " We have come to eat you, Hyas ! Hyas, we have come to eat you ! " and the earth would rumble and howl frightfully. "Hyas, Hyas, we will eat you!" Poor Hyas, what could he do? Suddenly he spied an eagle flying towards him. "Hey, grandfather," he cried, "can you help me?"

"What can I do, grandson?"

"Oh, grandfather, if you could hold up the string till the earth closes her mouth, I could jump across."

So Eagle swooped down and caught up the string of bones till the earth closed, and Hyas jumped across. After some days' travelling he came near his old home, and all the birds began singing, "Hyas tucksin! Hyas tucksin!" and making a great noise. The poor old mother of Hyas came out of the lodge and she heard them. "Alas!" said she, "where is my poor son to come from? He is dead this long while." But still the birds sang, "Hyas tucksin! Hyas tucksin!" Then Hyas looked, and there stood his mother, in rags and with scars of burns on her face. He ran forward and took her in his arms, crying: "Mother, I am here; look up. I have come back to you."

"My son, my son!" she cried for joy.

"Tell me how my father has treated you since I have been gone."

"Oh, I am a slave now, and they push me into the fire, and are very cruel to me."

"Now, I will be avenged," said Hyas. "Have they a young child?"

"Yes," said she.

"Well, you must go in and ask my father for some bear's grease for me, so that I may dress my hair, and if he refuses, ask to nurse the child, and make the fire red-hot, and then throw the child in and run out to me. I am going to punish them all."

Now, by this time all the people heard how Hyas came back, and his father came rushing out to see if it were true. Then, calling the people to .bring beaver and marten skins for Hyas to walk on.

"Tush!" said he, kicking the skins aside. "I have walked so far without them. Do I need them now?"

The father knew now that Hyas was greater than he, and that his bad spirits had been killed, and he was afraid. The mother asked for the bear's grease.

"Tish! No, indeed, I'll not give him any, so go and tell your son that he can do without."

So the poor old woman went to the child and took it to nurse it, as it was crying.

"Don't let her have the child," screamed the husband. "She means mischief."

"Let her have it," said the young mother, so the child was hushed by the old woman, who kept piling on the wood till the lodge was like a furnace. Then all at once she threw the child into the fire, and ran screaming to her son. He was waiting for her, and his father rushed out, but the fire had caught the lodge and burnt the inmates up. Then the village took fire and the people ran to their canoes. Hyas shot an arrow into the water and it began to boil, and their canoes were destroyed and they were drowned. Only Hyas and his mother were left alive. So he asked her what bird she would like to be, and she chose the lark, and she then became one; and Hyas turned into a beautiful red-breasted bird. So that was the end of all his travels and adventures.

INDEX.